MACHINES ★ AT WORK

BUSES

BY GARY M. AMOROSO AND CYNTHIA A. KLINGEL

THE CHILD'S WORLD® • MANKATO, MINNESOTA

The
Child's
World®

Published in the United States of America by The Child's World®
1980 Lookout Drive • Mankato, MN 56003-1705
800-599-READ • www.childsworld.com

PHOTO CREDITS
© Alan Schein Photography/Corbis: 15
© David Budd: cover, 2, 4, 7 (both), 12, 20
© Envision/Corbis: 8
© Kieran Doherty/Reuters/Corbis: 16
© iStockphoto.com/Andres Balcazar: 19
© iStockphoto.com/Jerry Horbert: 11
© Vicki France/BigStockPhoto.com: 3

ACKNOWLEDGMENTS
The Child's World®: Mary Berendes, Publishing Director;
Katherine Stevenson, Editor

The Design Lab: Kathleen Petelinsek, Design and Page Production

LIBRARY OF CONGRESS CATALOGING-IN-PUBLICATION DATA
Amoroso, Gary M.
  Buses / by Gary M. Amoroso and Cynthia A. Klingel.
    p. cm. — (Machines at work)
  Includes bibliographical references and index.
  ISBN 1-59296-827-9 (library bound : alk. paper)
  1. Buses—Juvenile literature. 2. Bus travel—Juvenile literature. I. Klingel, Cynthia Fitterer. II. Title. III. Series.
  TL232.A45 2006
  629.222'33—dc22   2006023283

Contents

Buses have a big door on the side.
Riders go up steps to get inside.

What are buses?

Buses are large **vehicles** that carry lots of people. There are many kinds of buses. Some buses carry people on long trips. Others carry them around town.

How do buses move?

Buses have a large **engine**. The engine makes power to turn the bus's wheels. The driver drives the bus just like a huge car. Inside, there are seats for **passengers**.

The small picture shows a bus driver at work. The big picture shows the seats for the passengers. There are a lot!

School buses stop often. They stay stopped while children climb the stairs. They do not go until the children sit down. ⭐

What are school buses like?

Many children ride school buses to and from school. They also ride them on school trips. Almost all school buses are yellow or orange. The colors make them easy to see.

School buses have yellow lights on the front and back. They have a stop sign on the side. When a school bus stops, its yellow lights flash. The stop sign sticks out. Other drivers must stop when they see these things.

The stop sign goes out when the driver opens the door.

COLORADO CHARTER LINES, INC.
ICC MC 145424 • CO PUC 11857
DENVER, COLORADO

storage

Motor coaches have big storage spaces underneath.

What are motor coaches like?

Motor coaches are big buses that travel between cities. A ride on a motor coach might last many hours. Motor coaches often have bathrooms. They have room for people's bags and suitcases. Some even have small movie screens!

13

What are city buses like?

City buses are used in many towns and cities. People ride them for short distances. The ride them to get to work. They ride them to go shopping or go to a movie. In many cities, taking the bus is easier than driving a car.

People pay money to ride on city buses. Some people ride them a lot. They get special cards to use each time.

This double-decker bus is in England. Which floor would you like to ride on?

What are double-decker buses like?

Double-decker buses have two floors. These buses hold many people. The riders can sit on either floor. Many countries have double-decker buses.

What are low-floor buses like?

Low-floor buses are a newer type of bus. They do not have steps. They are helpful for people who cannot climb steps.

18

STAND
CLEAR

DANGER
Do Not Stand in Stepwell
While Bus is in Motion.

People with wheelchairs or
scooters can use low-floor buses.

This motor coach is all clean and ready to go!

Are buses useful?

People all over the world ride buses. Some bus passengers do not have cars of their own. Others find buses quicker or easier than driving. Buses are very useful!

 # Glossary

coaches (KOH-chuz) "Coaches" is a name for some kinds of vehicles that carry people.

double-decker (DUH-bul DEH-kur) "Double-decker" means having two parts—one on top of the other.

engine (EN-jun) An engine is a machine that makes something move.

motor (MOH-tur) "Motor" is another name for an engine.

passengers (PA-sun-jurz) People who ride in something are called passengers.

vehicles (VEE-uh-kullz) Vehicles are things for carrying people or goods.

 # Books

Gorman, Jacqueline Laks. *Bus Driver/El conductor del autobús.* Milwaukee, WI: Weekly Reader Learning, 2002.

Oxlade, Chris. *Buses.* Oxford (England): Raintree, 2003.

Zuehlke, Jeffrey. *Buses.* Minneapolis, Lerner Publications, 2005.

 # Web Sites

Visit our Web site for lots of links about buses:
http://www.childsworld.com/links
Note to parents, teachers, and librarians: We routinely check our Web links to make sure they're safe, active sites—so encourage your readers to check them out!

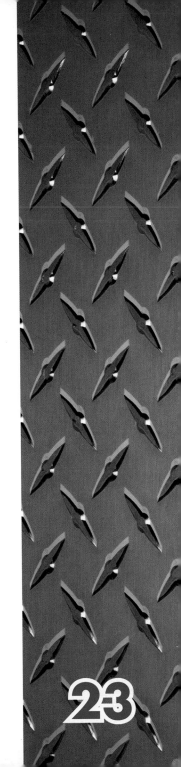

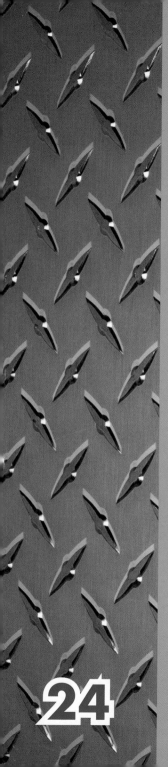

 # Index

 # About the Author

Gary M. Amoroso lives in Minnesota and enjoys traveling, sports, and having fun with friends and family. He has been a coach, teacher, principal, and district superintendent.

Cynthia A. Klingel is a Director of Curriculum and Instruction in a Minnesota school district. She enjoys reading, writing, gardening, traveling, and spending time with friends and family.